DIVISION
WIPE-OFF FUN

Watermill Press

Printed in the United States of America.

10 9 8 7 6

HOW TO USE DIVISION FUN

Say each number fact aloud. After you have memorized each set of facts, place the wipe-off fold from the back cover over the answers. Then use a grease pencil to write the answers in the boxes provided.

When you are all done, lift the fold to check your answers. Then use a dry or wet tissue or paper towel to wipe off the answers. You can use each page again and again for learning-time fun!

One

1

$4 \div 1 = 4$

$10 \div 1 = 10$

$6 \div 1 = 6$

$8 \div 1 = 8$

$12 \div 1 = 12$

$2 \div 1 = 2$

$3 \div 1 = 3$

$11 \div 1 = 11$

$5 \div 1 = 5$

$1 \div 1 = 1$

$9 \div 1 = 9$

$7 \div 1 = 7$

SON: I studied math for two hours last night, and I still failed today's test.

FATHER: Why?

SON: The test was in social studies!

Two

2

14 ÷ 2 = 7

6 ÷ 2 = 3

2 ÷ 2 = 1

24 ÷ 2 = 12

10 ÷ 2 = 5

18 ÷ 2 = 9

8 ÷ 2 = 4

22 ÷ 2 = 11

16 ÷ 2 = 8

4 ÷ 2 = 2

20 ÷ 2 = 10

12 ÷ 2 = 6

Why is the moon like a dollar?

It has four quarters!

Three

3

15 ÷ 3 = 5

6 ÷ 3 = 2

36 ÷ 3 = 12

9 ÷ 3 = 3

27 ÷ 3 = 9

18 ÷ 3 = 6

3 ÷ 3 = 1

24 ÷ 3 = 8

12 ÷ 3 = 4

21 ÷ 3 = 7

30 ÷ 3 = 10

33 ÷ 3 = 11

How can you get 45 using only 4, 4, 4, and 4?
(You can't add, subtract, multiply, or divide.)

44 4/4.

Four

4

48 ÷ 4 = 12

36 ÷ 4 = 9

16 ÷ 4 = 4

4 ÷ 4 = 1

20 ÷ 4 = 5

44 ÷ 4 = 11

12 ÷ 4 = 3

32 ÷ 4 = 8

8 ÷ 4 = 2

40 ÷ 4 = 10

28 ÷ 4 = 7

24 ÷ 4 = 6

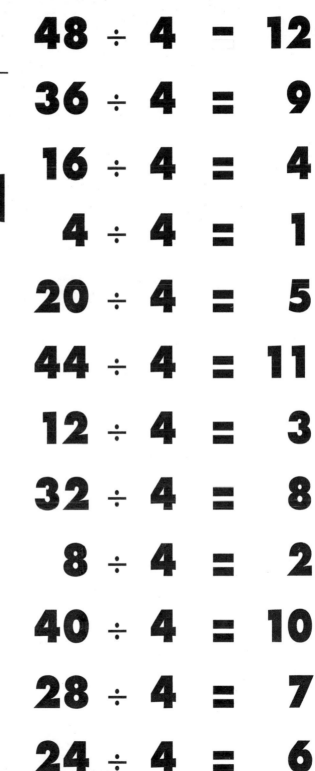

If you had 5 potatoes and had to divide them equally between 3 people, what should you do first?

Mash them!

Five

5

30 ÷ 5 = 6

50 ÷ 5 = 10

45 ÷ 5 = 9

15 ÷ 5 = 3

55 ÷ 5 = 11

25 ÷ 5 = 5

5 ÷ 5 = 1

20 ÷ 5 = 4

10 ÷ 5 = 2

35 ÷ 5 = 7

40 ÷ 5 = 8

60 ÷ 5 = 12

One boy has 9 piles of hay, and another has 21 piles of hay. How many piles of hay do they have altogether?

One big pile!

Six

6

18 ÷ 6 = 3

54 ÷ 6 = 9

66 ÷ 6 = 11

24 ÷ 6 = 4

30 ÷ 6 = 5

6 ÷ 6 = 1

72 ÷ 6 = 12

36 ÷ 6 = 6

12 ÷ 6 = 2

60 ÷ 6 = 10

48 ÷ 6 = 8

42 ÷ 6 = 7

If 5 cats catch 5 mice in 5 minutes, how long will it take one cat to catch a mouse?

Five minutes.

Seven

7

49	÷	7	=	7
21	÷	7	=	3
35	÷	7	=	5
77	÷	7	=	11
14	÷	7	=	2
70	÷	7	=	10
28	÷	7	=	4
56	÷	7	=	8
84	÷	7	=	12
7	÷	7	=	1
42	÷	7	=	6
63	÷	7	=	9

If you put 6 ducks in a carton, what do you get?

A box of quackers!

Eight

8

40 ÷ 8 = 5

96 ÷ 8 = 12

8 ÷ 8 = 1

56 ÷ 8 = 7

32 ÷ 8 = 4

16 ÷ 8 = 2

80 ÷ 8 = 10

48 ÷ 8 = 6

24 ÷ 8 = 3

88 ÷ 8 = 11

72 ÷ 8 = 9

64 ÷ 8 = 8

How can you make the number 7 even?

Take away the letter S!

Nine

9

99 ÷ 9 = 11

45 ÷ 9 = 5

18 ÷ 9 = 2

72 ÷ 9 = 8

36 ÷ 9 = 4

9 ÷ 9 = 1

81 ÷ 9 = 9

108 ÷ 9 = 12

54 ÷ 9 = 6

90 ÷ 9 = 10

63 ÷ 9 = 7

27 ÷ 9 = 3

TEACHER: Use the word *geometry* in a sentence.
STUDENT: The little acorn grew and grew, and one day it woke up and said, "Gee, ahm-a-tree!"

Ten

10

$30 \div 10 = 3$

$60 \div 10 = 6$

$80 \div 10 = 8$

$20 \div 10 = 2$

$110 \div 10 = 11$

$50 \div 10 = 5$

$70 \div 10 = 7$

$10 \div 10 = 1$

$100 \div 10 = 10$

$120 \div 10 = 12$

$90 \div 10 = 9$

$40 \div 10 = 4$

There were 99 people on a boat. It turned over.
How many were left?

˙99

Eleven

11

$22 \div 11 = 2$

$110 \div 11 = 10$

$99 \div 11 = 9$

$55 \div 11 = 5$

$11 \div 11 = 1$

$66 \div 11 = 6$

$132 \div 11 = 12$

$33 \div 11 = 3$

$77 \div 11 = 7$

$44 \div 11 = 4$

$88 \div 11 = 8$

$121 \div 11 = 11$

How can you divide 4 apples among 5 people?

Make applesauce!